James Lafayette

Black Hero of the American Revolution

by

Glenda Armand

Voices in History: Biography Series™

ISBN 978-1-68380-902-9

COPYRIGHT © 2023 CORE KNOWLEDGE FOUNDATION

ALL RIGHTS RESERVED

PRINTED IN CANADA

EDITORIAL DIRECTOR:
Rosie McCormick

CORE KNOWLEDGE FOUNDATION

801 EAST HIGH STREET

CHARLOTTESVILLE, VIRGINIA 22902

www.coreknowledge.org

TABLE OF CONTENTS

Introduction

The United States of America began as thirteen colonies situated along the east coast of the North American continent. The colonies were built on land that had been occupied for thousands of years by Indigenous people. Amid ever-present conflict and some cooperation with these native inhabitants, the colonies were founded by immigrants from Europe. Most of them were from England, a country on the island of Great Britain, but a number of the colonists came from other countries, such as Scotland, France, and Germany.

Africans made up the second-largest group of people living in the colonies. Unlike the European colonists, most of the Africans were brought to America against their will and forced into slavery. All of the colonists—white and black, enslaved and free—were subjects of the king of Great Britain and Ireland. And life in the colonies reflected British culture. But as time passed, the colonists began to feel less and less connected to the mother country. By 1763, it was not uncommon for colonists to describe themselves as American.

After all, the mother country was on the other side of the Atlantic Ocean, more than three thousand miles away. It was part of the Old World. Why pledge allegiance to a distant king? Why should the king make the laws for a land he would never set foot on?

Time passed, and the colonists became rebellious. They protested the king and his rule. King George III, who had been crowned in 1760, sent red-coated soldiers to discipline his unruly American "children." His soldiers would easily silence these protests—or so the king thought. But the American colonists would not be silenced.

The colonists fought the Redcoats. They started a war, which became a revolution.

During the American Revolution, some black colonists, enslaved and free, chose to fight on the side of the Americans. They believed that American independence would bring freedom to black people, too. And so they fought heroically.

Among the black heroes of the revolution was a man who is still largely unknown. Yet he risked his life in service to the new nation. In doing so, he came into contact with legendary figures whom history will never forget—George Washington, Lord Cornwallis, Benedict Arnold, and the Marquis de Lafayette.

It is possible that without this one man's knowledge, skill, and bravery, the ragtag Continental army never would have defeated the most powerful military on Earth. This remarkable man was born into slavery. And he had just one name—James.

1

Born into Slavery

Fourteen-year-old James repeated the French words after the tutor: *"Bonjour, mon ami."*

When the other student, William Armistead, said the same words, which meant "Hello, my friend," the tutor heaped him with praise. James knew that his own pronunciation had been better. But that did not matter. When the tutor came to the plantation in New Kent County, Virginia, it was not for James but for William. James did not expect praise. The reason was simple: William was the plantation owner's son. James was the owner's slave.

William's father, John Armistead, had given James a job to do. He was to be young William's companion and playmate. James was to eat meals with him and attend lessons with him. Yet James must never forget that even though he was a few years older than William, it was James's duty to obey William or be punished—perhaps with a whip.

James had been born on the Armistead tobacco plantation in 1748. Before he was chosen to be William's companion, James lived like other enslaved children on a southern plantation. Always hungry, young enslaved children wore simple shifts—shapeless frocks—or nothing at all. They began working around the age of three. They collected trash, fed the chickens, and shooed away birds from the gardens.

James knew how fortunate he was. Once he became William's playmate, his stomach no longer growled. He wore better clothes and had fewer chores. And most important of all, he was tutored alongside William in reading, writing, arithmetic, and French. Most enslaved people were not taught to read and write. And James knew why.

A slave who could write could forge a pass that would make it easier to escape to freedom in the North. A slave who could read could learn about abolition and slave rebellions and encourage other enslaved people to rebel. To most slave owners, an educated slave was a dangerous slave.

So James learned as much as he could as fast as he could. At any time, William might decide that he no longer wanted James as his friend. That would mean no more eating until he was full. No more clean, well-fitting clothes. No more lessons.

If that happened, James might be forced to work in the tobacco fields with the adults, six days a week, sunup to sundown. James knew what it took to grow the highly prized plant. He saw how the field hands spent hours on end bent over and tending the tobacco seedlings.

When the tobacco was ripe, it was often attacked by caterpillars called "tobacco worms." These mean-looking horned creatures were as long as a man's thumb. James had watched the laborers carefully pick the destructive pests off the plants without tearing the tobacco leaves, which were easily torn. While the workers performed this backbreaking chore, an overseer followed closely behind them, checking their work. Because the caterpillars were the same green color as the leaves they ate, the pests were easily overlooked. Sometimes a cruel overseer forced a worker to eat a tobacco worm he had missed.

No, James did not look forward to working in the tobacco fields.

There were other jobs to do on the plantation—blacksmithing, carpentry, tending the stables. As James spent less time with William, he spent more time learning and doing those other jobs. Whatever job he performed, he did well. That way, he avoided the whip—or an even worse punishment: being separated from his family and sold to a plantation owner farther south.

James had heard that in the colonies of Georgia and North and South Carolina, life for enslaved people was more <u>abysmal</u> than it was in the colony of Virginia. The sun beat down on them mercilessly as they picked cotton and sowed rice. And the overseers were even crueler. Knowing that life could be much worse, James lived in constant dread of what might happen.

The plantation owner's son had no such worries. Young William did not have to fear being whipped or sold or forced to eat a worm. James thought it was unfair that white people were allowed to "own" black people. Like William, he wanted to grow up and make decisions for himself. He wanted to choose the work he performed. And if he worked for someone else, he wanted to be paid for that work. James vowed that he would do whatever it took to be the master of his own fate. To be free.

abysmal: extremely bad

2

Whose Revolution?

When he became an adult, James worked as a clerk for William Armistead, his former playmate. Still enslaved, James kept track of William's many business dealings. As he worked, James eavesdropped on lively conversations between William and the people with whom he did business. The men took no notice of James as they argued about the price of tobacco or whether there would be a bumper crop that year.

James did not know it then, but his knack for listening in on others' conversations while going unnoticed would come in handy one day.

Soon, those conversations turned from farming to politics. The men spoke of tensions between the thirteen colonies and England, the mother country. These tensions kept building. King George III began imposing new tax laws on the colonies.

James kept up with the news and gossip as the colonists became angrier and angrier with each new law. They refused to pay the taxes. They <u>boycotted</u> British goods. They destroyed British property. They tarred and feathered customs officers sent by the king.

The actions of the colonists convinced George III that he needed to send troops to the colonies to maintain order. In 1768, he sent four thousand red-coated soldiers to Boston, a city located in the northern colony of Massachusetts. The Bostonians resented the presence of the Redcoats. To add to their displeasure, the people of Boston were forced to provide the British soldiers with food and public places where they could take shelter.

Although the Massachusetts colony was the center of the clash between the British and the colonists, all thirteen colonies were forced to pay taxes and submit to laws they felt were unjust.

James listened as William and his peers got into heated debates about taxes and the presence of British troops in Boston. He wondered what this dispute between white colonists and their mother country could mean for himself and his fellow enslaved people.

James even heard rumors that the colonies might

---

boycotted: refused to buy

break away from Great Britain—that they might join together and create a new nation. To James, that brought to mind a question: could people who wanted freedom for themselves continue to enslave other people?

James learned that on March 5, 1770, a rowdy group of colonists had thrown snowballs, shells, and coal at some British soldiers. The crowd taunted the soldiers, calling them "lobsterbacks" because of their bright red, long-tailed jackets, daring them to shoot. In the confusion, one of the soldiers was struck, and whether by accident or on purpose, he discharged his musket. Other soldiers then fired their guns too. Five members of the crowd were shot and killed. This incident became known as the Boston Massacre.

This was followed by the Boston Tea Party on December 16, 1773. This was not a real tea party. Instead, a group of colonists disguised themselves as Native Americans and dumped British tea into the Boston Harbor rather than pay taxes on it.

On April 19, 1775, minutemen, or citizens who were ready to do battle on short notice, fought the British at the Battles of Lexington and Concord in Massachusetts. Those battles marked the beginning of the American Revolution.

When the revolution began, James was twenty-seven years old and still determined to be free. He, like other black colonists, wondered what this war would mean for them. Would it lead to freedom?

In June 1775, the Continental Congress decided to bring together under one leader all the militias and volunteer soldiers fighting the British. Because of his military experience, the Congress chose the Virginian George Washington to be the commander in chief of the new Continental army.

So far, the fighting had yet to reach the southern colonies. True, Virginians were boycotting British goods, but would they take up arms against the mightiest military in the world? Then, on October 26, 1775, the war reached the South. British and Continental soldiers exchanged gunfire at Hampton, Virginia. The Battle of

Hampton lasted less than a day, but it brought the war within fifty miles of James's home.

Now Virginians would have to choose a side. Neighbors argued with neighbors. Families were torn apart.

Would they be Loyalists and declare their allegiance to the king?

"We are Englishmen!" some colonists shouted.

Or would they be Patriots and root for independence?

"We are Americans!" insisted others.

James had only one question: which side would offer freedom to black people?

3

A Chance to Be Free

On November 7, 1775, the Earl of Dunmore, the British royal governor of Virginia, proclaimed that enslaved men who volunteered to serve in the king's army would be granted their freedom. What a tempting <u>proposition</u>! Less than a month after Dunmore's proclamation, three hundred black men had left their plantations and signed up to fight for the king.

James wondered if this might be his only chance to escape from slavery. He knew that General George Washington, a Virginia slaveholder himself, had barred all black people from serving in the Continental army. Washington, like many slaveholders, feared that armed black men would turn their weapons on the slaveholders.

However, James had a family to consider. This made the decision harder. Would the British free his family too? What if the British lost the war? What would happen to all those who had been promised freedom? James would have to make a decision soon. Events were moving fast.

---

proposition: offer

Even though Dunmore's proclamation was intended only for Virginia's enslaved men, it echoed throughout the southern colonies. From Maryland to Georgia, thousands of enslaved men escaped to join the British army. The British welcomed them. They trained the black recruits to work as guides, dig trenches, chop down trees, and clear roads.

General Washington struggled with how to respond to Dunmore's proclamation. On July 4, 1776, after more than a year of fighting, the Continental Congress had declared that the thirteen colonies were now independent states. Washington knew that the king would not simply give the Americans their independence. They would have to fight harder than ever—and Washington was having trouble recruiting men. He realized that refusing to recruit black men had been a mistake. He would have to trust black Americans, knowing that they had the same cause as white Americans—freedom. In 1777, General Washington gave his approval to the states to recruit black men, both enslaved and free, by promising freedom to enslaved men who joined the Continental army.

When James heard the news, he was working at another job for William. When the war began, William Armistead had been appointed as a commissary, or official in charge, of military supplies for Virginia's armory.

The armory was a store that provided guns, ammunition, and other items that the Continental army needed. To perform this job, William traveled to Williamsburg, Virginia, where the armory was located. He brought James with him to be his assistant.

Working in the armory and traveling between New Kent County and Williamsburg allowed James the opportunity to witness the war as it unfolded. He saw hundreds of British and American soldiers passing through the countryside. The soldiers searched the region, looking for food for the men and <u>fodder</u> for their horses. The British army paid Loyalist farmers for the items they took. However, they stole from Patriots. The Continental army did just the opposite—paying the Patriots and stealing from the Loyalists.

James caught sight of many men who had escaped slavery and joined the British army. They would rather suffer the wounds of war than those caused by whips and chains. The black soldiers proudly donned uniforms that bore the inscription "Liberty to Slaves." Should he join the British army? James wondered.

> **Time to Make a Choice**
>
> *Despite new legislation passed by the states that would free enslaved men who enlisted, the majority of black men chose to fight on the side of the British. Many chose not to fight on the side of the people who had enslaved them.*

fodder: livestock food

4

James and the Marquis de Lafayette

In 1780, the Virginia armory was moved to the town of Richmond. William Armistead and James went with it. While working in the armory, James met a French general who was fighting on the side of the Patriots. France had been sending supplies to the colonists for their fight for independence almost since the beginning of the war. But after France and Great Britain declared war against each other in 1778, the French sent troops and warships as well to help the Americans fight their mutual enemy.

Some Frenchmen, like the young general James met, also volunteered their services. The general had the incredibly long name of Marie-Joseph Paul Yves Roch Gilbert du Motier, Marquis de Lafayette. Americans called him the Marquis de Lafayette or simply Lafayette.

The Anglo-French War

This war was fought between Great Britain and the Kingdom of France between 1778 and 1783. It began when France formed an alliance (friendship) with the thirteen colonies during the American Revolution. France and Great Britain fought over control of the English Channel, the Mediterranean Sea, the Indian Ocean, and the West Indies. The war ended with a French victory.

James was impressed by this wealthy young foreigner who had come to the United States in 1777, when he, Lafayette, was only nineteen years old. When he first arrived, Lafayette had no military experience and spoke little English. By the time James met him in the spring of 1781, the twenty-three-year-old Frenchman spoke fluent English and had become commander of a division of the Continental army. General Lafayette and his 1,200 troops were now stationed in nearby Williamsburg, Virginia.

General Lafayette was a frequent visitor to the armory. He was always trying to improve the condition of his troops. Lafayette often used his own money to buy shoes and clothing for his men.

Here, thought James, was a man who was willing to give his life for a foreign nation. Lafayette, James marveled, was a white man who believed that white and black people were equal—that all people deserved liberty. The Frenchman was strongly opposed to slavery.

James had never met a man like Marie-Joseph Paul Yves Roch Gilbert du Motier, Marquis de Lafayette.

5

James Chooses a Side

James had gotten to know General Lafayette very well, so he was quite interested when the general declared that he wanted to recruit four hundred black men for his unit. The new recruits would be laborers and wagoners.

James trusted General Lafayette. Surely, if he joined the Patriots under Lafayette's command, he would be rewarded with <u>emancipation</u>.

With that in mind, James went to William Armistead and told him that he wanted to fight for his country's independence and for his own freedom. Grateful that James had chosen the Patriot side, William gave James permission to join the Continental army.

emancipation: freedom from another's control

In March 1781, James, thirty-three years old and yearning to be free, said goodbye to William, and put his fate in the hands of the twenty-three-year-old Marquis de Lafayette.

6

James the Spy

When James offered his services to Lafayette, the Frenchman was overjoyed. James was smart. He could read and write, and he knew the Virginia landscape. Lafayette decided that James would not be a laborer or wagoner. No, the Frenchman had bigger plans for James. He asked James if he would become a spy.

Dangerous Work

Espionage was practiced by both the British and Continental armies. Spies were essential. They could let their officers know how many men the other side had ready for battle. They could say when and where the enemy planned to attack. Spies could make the difference between winning and losing a battle. But spying was a dangerous job. Because each side engaged in espionage, both sides were always on the lookout for spies sent by the enemy. One slipup, one telltale look or careless comment, could cause the spy to be discovered. And if discovered, the spy would be put to death immediately.

Espionage: spying to get information about the other side

For the British and the Americans, recruiting runaway slaves as spies made sense. Both sides believed that black people owed no loyalty to the Patriots or the Loyalists. They thought that enslaved people had no interest in who won the war.

But James did have an interest in who won the war. This was his country too. This was where he had been born. This was where he wanted to raise his family and live out his life. He was a Virginian and an American—and he wanted to be free. If soldiers were worthy of emancipation, how much worthier would a spy be? For the first time, James believed that he would soon be a free man.

"Yes," James responded to General Lafayette, "I will become a spy."

Soon General Lafayette gave James his first mission, He was to spy on Benedict Arnold, the most infamous <u>traitor</u> in American history.

---

traitor: one who betrays the trust of a person or country

7

James and Benedict Arnold

When the revolution began, Benedict Arnold was on the side of the Patriots. He was well liked by George Washington and had fought bravely in many battles. But by 1779, General Arnold had begun to feel unappreciated. Other officers were given promotions that Arnold believed he had earned. His resentment grew so strong that Benedict Arnold decided to switch sides. He would fight for the British!

General George Washington was now his enemy. At first, Arnold stayed with the Continental army and passed on information to the British. But he was soon discovered. He fled to the British army before he could be caught and hanged as a spy.

The British welcomed the turncoat. Benedict Arnold could breathe a little easier. He was a wanted man, but now he had the king's army to protect him. Arnold was made a general in the British army. General Arnold invaded Virginia in January 1781 with 1,600 men.

He and his men wreaked <u>havoc</u> on the state. They raided the Patriots' military supplies. They <u>ransacked</u> farms; burned towns, ships, and warehouses full of tobacco; and seized weapons. They set plantations on fire. The American troops were too few in number to stop them.

Lafayette wanted nothing more than to capture Benedict Arnold. Could James gather information that would help Patriot soldiers capture the traitor?

James agreed to try. He donned tattered clothes and walked to the camp of Benedict Arnold. James told the sentries guarding the entrance that he had run away from his master and wanted to serve in the British army. James stood, unflinching as the soldiers looked him over. Would they believe his story?

It made sense to them. The shoeless black man seemed to be just who he said he was—a runaway slave. At last, the soldiers waved James in. He had passed his first test! He was now an official spy for the Continental army. And he was in the camp of Benedict Arnold.

James was immediately put to work. He labored alongside the other black men in the camp. Working as a forager, he searched for provisions and fodder in fields and farms to feed the royal army.

havoc: widespread destruction
ransacked: searched and robbed destructively

He also guided British soldiers along roads that he knew like the back of his hand. By leading the Redcoats through Virginia, James was able to gather information about where they were headed next.

James found out that he was not the only American spy behind enemy lines. Once he discovered who the other spies were, he and they were able to secretly exchange information. James relayed secrets, such as troop movements, to General Lafayette by note or by word of mouth from one spy to another. At other times, James walked back to Lafayette's camp with the information himself.

Lafayette was pleased with the information that he received from James. Still, he wanted the main prize—the capture of Benedict Arnold. To get information about when General Arnold would be unguarded, James would have to get inside the tent that served as Arnold's headquarters. But how would he do that? As it happened, James soon got his chance.

General Arnold asked one of his lieutenants to choose one of the black men in his camp to serve as his personal assistant. The lieutenant chose one of the men he felt to be hardworking and skillful. He chose James.

What luck! Now James was just where he needed to be—inside Benedict Arnold's tent. James washed Arnold's uniforms. He served his meals. He squashed mosquitoes that had wandered inside the tent. As James performed these <u>menial</u> tasks, he listened to every word the general uttered.

menial: lowly

Fortunately, General Arnold spoke freely in front of James. It was as if James were invisible to him. One day, James overheard Arnold tell a lieutenant that he was going to spend some time alone in the woods that night. Arnold told the lieutenant where he would be. The quick-tempered general made it clear that he was not to be disturbed unless it was a dire emergency.

As soon as he could, James gave this crucial information to a fellow spy. The spy relayed the message to Lafayette, who sent soldiers to the spot where Benedict Arnold would be. It looked like Lafayette was finally going to capture his <u>nemesis</u>.

That night, Lafayette's soldiers spotted Arnold alone just outside the northeast end of the British army camp. As General Arnold gazed upon the water of a moonlit pond, the soldiers sneaked up on him. The traitor was almost within reach when one of the soldiers stepped on a twig.

Snap!

Arnold turned and saw his would-be captors. He ran and hid in the foliage until the soldiers gave up the search and left. When Arnold got back to his tent, he was furious. There was a spy in the camp, and he must be captured and hanged!

---

nemesis: enemy or rival

8

James and Lord Cornwallis

Benedict Arnold never found out who had alerted Lafayette to his whereabouts. It never occurred to him that it had been James.

In fact, when General Arnold's superiors ordered him and his men to leave Virginia and head north, Arnold recommended James to another British general who was stationed in Virginia—Charles, Lord Cornwallis.

General Cornwallis was familiar with James. As General Arnold's assistant, James had followed Arnold as he moved between British camps. Cornwallis was happy to have James's services. The general quickly put the "runaway slave" to work as his personal assistant.

James was in a perfect position to continue his espionage. Like Benedict Arnold, General Cornwallis took no notice of his assistant as he went about his chores. Cornwallis assumed that James had no interest in or understanding of what he and the other British officers were discussing. He also believed that James could not read. That proved to be a costly mistake.

When Cornwallis had other officers over for dinner to talk strategy, James waited on their table. He listened intently as the officers reviewed secret plans. James read maps and documents. He learned the number of troops and weapons Cornwallis had. He found out where Cornwallis would move his troops next and where and when attacks would take place. Later, when he was alone, James wrote down what he had learned and delivered it to other spies, who then gave the secrets to General Lafayette.

Lafayette was grateful for the intelligence. It was just the kind of information that General George Washington needed. Lafayette let Washington know that the secrets he was passing on had been gathered by an "honest friend."

9

His Name Has Greatly Troubled My Sleep

Even though General Lafayette tried to keep his forces strong, as General Washington had ordered, the young general's forces were greatly outnumbered by Cornwallis's. When Cornwallis brought his troops to Virginia, he had combined them with the British troops that were already there. That brought the enemy's total strength to 7,000 men. Lafayette had only 3,200 men.

So with the information James provided about Cornwallis's plans, Lafayette could do little more than harass the experienced British general. Rather than do battle, Lafayette had his soldiers shadow Cornwallis and his men, threatening and hounding them. The Frenchman hoped that this would trick Cornwallis into thinking that the Continental army was eager to fight.

Even as he provoked Cornwallis, Lafayette knew he could not keep it up forever. He wondered how he could ever hope to defeat Cornwallis's army. "This devil

Cornwallis is much wiser than the other generals with whom I have dealt," Lafayette wrote in a letter to his brother-in-law on July 9, 1781. "He inspires me with a sincere fear, and his name has greatly troubled my sleep."

Without more men and more weapons, a victory against Cornwallis seemed impossible. However, shortly after he wrote the letter to his brother-in-law, Lafayette received the most important message he had ever received from James. General Cornwallis, wrote James, was moving his troops and would set up camp in Yorktown, along the Chesapeake Bay. There, Cornwallis and his men would await reinforcements. The British ships would be carrying much-needed weapons and ammunition. And they would bring an additional ten thousand troops.

Ten thousand troops! Certainly that would spell doom for the Americans. But Lafayette also saw some good news in the note from James. The Frenchman knew Yorktown well. Cornwallis was about to set up his camp on a peninsula. Cornwallis and his men would be almost surrounded by water, with only one escape route by land. If both escape routes could be blocked, then Lafayette could back Cornwallis into a corner.

For that to happen, the Americans would need perfect timing and a great deal of luck. It was a long shot. But it gave Lafayette hope for the first time in a long while. And he slept just a little bit better.

10

James the Double Agent

In the meantime, James continued his duties as Lafayette's spy and Cornwallis's personal assistant. Shortly after James sent Lafayette the message about Cornwallis's plan to move his men to Yorktown, Cornwallis summoned James. The general told James that he had something very important to talk to him about.

Oh, no, James thought, *I have been discovered*. He prepared himself for the worst.

To James's relief, Cornwallis began by praising him for carrying out his duties faithfully and efficiently. James thanked the general. Cornwallis continued. He was so impressed with James that he had a special job for him. What could that be? James wondered.

Cornwallis asked James if he would be willing to become a spy for the British. James was shocked, but he did not show it. Obviously, Cornwallis had no idea that James was already a spy—for the Americans.

James immediately saw the opportunity that had just been presented to him. As he pondered Cornwallis's request, James thought back to when he was a little boy. He had vowed to do whatever it took to be free. But never in his wildest dreams had he imagined this! And even as he gave Cornwallis his answer, James could not know that his decision would play a decisive role in the outcome of the war.

James returned to General Lafayette's camp in Williamsburg with the incredible news. He had agreed to be a spy for General Cornwallis. Lafayette immediately understood. Of course, James was not really going to spy for Cornwallis. If he were, he certainly would not tell Lafayette! James planned to *pretend* to spy for Cornwallis while actually spying for Lafayette.

Lafayette assured James that he did not have to do it. Being a double agent meant double the danger. It would mean that in addition to delivering British secrets to the Americans, James would be giving false information to the British. What if British soldiers discovered James bringing their secret plans to the Americans? They would hang him immediately. What if he were stopped by American soldiers who did not know that what he was carrying to the British was <u>misinformation</u>? He would meet the same fate.

---

misinformation: incorrect information

Yet Lafayette had to admit that the timing was perfect for James to become a double agent. After six years of war, both the British and Continental armies were exhausted.

Back in Great Britain, the war was unpopular. The British had gained control of only a few territories. And at the same time they were fighting in America, the British were also at war with France and Spain. What the British had thought would be a simple act of "disciplining unruly children" had turned into a full-fledged war with no end in sight.

The Price of War

For Americans, the struggle for independence led to shortages of money, food, and weapons. Continental soldiers were tired, hungry, and often unpaid. Both sides were desperate for the war to end.

Lafayette believed that with James's help, the war could end soon with an American victory. Still, if James did not want to go through with this dangerous mission, Lafayette would understand. He would give James another assignment and never send him back to Cornwallis's camp. But James had made up his mind. He would take the risk. He would be a double agent.

11

James, George Washington, and the Battle of Yorktown

James began his dangerous dual role right away. He soon informed General Lafayette that Cornwallis was preparing for battle. That was bad news. Lafayette was still not ready to take on Cornwallis. So with James's help, Lafayette came up with a ploy.

Lafayette wrote an official-looking order for General Daniel Morgan to bring his troops to Virginia to join forces with Lafayette's. General Morgan and his men were admired by the Americans and feared by the British. They were known for their fierce fighting tactics and their deadly accuracy with a new weapon called a rifle.

After writing the note, Lafayette tore the paper and handed the pieces to James.

---

tactics: methods

James returned to the British camp and presented the torn note to General Cornwallis. James made up a story that he had found the torn pieces of paper along the road. Keeping up the pretense that he was illiterate, James told Cornwallis that he did not know if the note was important. Cornwallis put the pieces together, read the fake note, and assured James that it was indeed important. Cornwallis did not want to do battle with General Morgan, so he called off the attack. Once again, James's services had proven to be invaluable to the Americans.

The American rifle

The American rifle was first used for hunting. It had an unusually long barrel. During the Revolutionary War, the Continental Congress formed ten rifle units. Colonel Daniel Morgan's rifle unit was the first. Morgan's sharpshooters and their long rifles began picking off anyone in a red uniform.

This was the first time British troops had ever come across such a weapon. They did not know what to make of it. "The Redcoats are so amazingly terrified by our riflemen," one soldier reportedly said, "that they will not stir beyond their lines."

Most American soldiers would not have known what to do with a long rifle. Morgan's sharpshooters were experts with their weapons because rifle marksmanship was a part of their way of life.

Warfare History Network

Now that Cornwallis was no longer planning to attack, General Lafayette could focus on the scheme that he and General Washington were devising. Lafayette had been in constant correspondence with Washington, who was fighting battles up north in New York. The two generals continued planning what would come to be known as the Battle of Yorktown.

Two weeks after Cornwallis and his men had begun occupying Yorktown, General Washington had received great news. French admiral François de Grasse was sailing for Chesapeake Bay with a fleet of twenty-eight battleships and a three-thousand-man army. Could Admiral de Grasse reach the Chesapeake before the British ships carrying ten thousand soldiers?

Knowing that the French fleet was on its way, General Washington joined his forces with those of another French general, Jean-Baptiste Rochambeau. Together, they began secretly moving their army of almost eight thousand men south to Yorktown. Would they arrive in time?

On August 30, the French fleet arrived at Chesapeake Bay. They had beaten the British to the bay! The French ships delivered much-needed supplies and soldiers to the Marquis de Lafayette. When the British fleet arrived, Admiral de Grasse's fleet blocked the British ships from entering the bay.

On September 28, American and French soldiers under the command of Generals Washington and Rochambeau arrived at Yorktown.

On October 9, the combined American and French forces, totaling 16,650 men, began bombarding the British camp around the clock.

Now General Cornwallis and his men were surrounded, outmanned, outgunned, and running low on food. They could not escape. No help could reach them by sea. The British surrendered to General George Washington on October 19, 1781.

The battle had gone exactly as planned. Weather, timing, and luck had all been in the Continental army's favor. Though James did not fight in the battle, the information he provided had set in motion the events that would lead to the astounding victory. General Washington, who would become the first president of the United States of America, knew that it would not have been possible if not for the information he had received from Lafayette's "honest friend," James.

12

A Cruel Surprise

Two days after he surrendered, General Cornwallis requested a meeting with General Lafayette. When he entered Lafayette's headquarters, Cornwallis was amazed to see the black man he had believed to be his spy.

"Ah, you rogue," Cornwallis said to James, "then you have been playing me a trick all this time."

The Battle of Yorktown was the last great battle of the American Revolution. James's career as a spy also ended when General Cornwallis surrendered on that autumn day in 1781.

James said goodbye to his friend the Marquis de Lafayette.

"Au revoir," replied Lafayette, reminding James that there were two words for *goodbye* in French. *Au revoir* meant they would see each other again. *Adieu* meant goodbye forever. Promising that he would return, Lafayette left for France in December 1781.

James believed that it was now just a matter of time before he would receive his manumission, or release from slavery, papers. As it turned out, James was in for a cruel surprise.

As promised, after the United States won the war, enslaved men who had served in the military were emancipated. In Virginia, a law was passed that read in part:

Whereas . . . all persons enlisted . . . who have . . . contributed towards the establishment of American liberty and independence, should enjoy the blessings of freedom as a reward for their toils and labours; *Be it therefore enacted*, That each and every slave, who . . . hath enlisted in any regiment or corps raised within this state . . . shall from and after the passing of this act, be fully and compleatly emancipated, and shall be held and deemed free . . . as if each and every one of them were specially named in this act.

However, James had not "enlisted in any regiment or corps." He had not been a soldier. And to his utter dismay, he was told that the law did not apply to him. It did not say anything about spies receiving their freedom. And so, despite having risked his life to help the United States win independence, James was still a slave.

13

As If He Had Been Born Free

Even though he returned to William Armistead still enslaved, James did not give up. He would not rest until he was a free man. He <u>petitioned</u> the Virginia legislature for his freedom. He argued that his services during the revolution were equal to those of a soldier. Again and again, his petitions were denied or ignored. Just when James might have given up hope, help arrived.

Although the Battle of Yorktown had marked the end of the fighting, the war was not declared over at that time. It would be two years before the American Revolutionary War officially ended, with a peace treaty that was signed in Paris, France, on September 3, 1783.

The Marquis de Lafayette had helped write the treaty. After the treaty was signed, Lafayette, true to his word, returned to the United States, his adopted country, in 1784–85. He visited all thirteen states. In New York,

---

petitioned: formally requested in writing

he assisted with peace talks between the new nation and the Iroquois people. In Richmond, Virginia, he gave a speech before the House of Delegates in which he demanded "liberty of all mankind" and argued for the emancipation of all people who were enslaved.

While he was in Virginia, Lafayette visited his dear friend James. When he found out that James was still enslaved, Lafayette was furious: "I never would have drawn my sword in the cause of America, if I could have conceived that thereby I was helping to found a nation of slaves."

Before he returned to France, the marquis penned a letter on James's behalf. James thanked him, and once again, the two men said *au revoir*.

Testimonial by Marquis de Lafayette on Behalf of James

This is to certify that the bearer by the name of James has done essential services to me while I had the honour to command in this state. His intelligences from the enemy's camp were industriously collected and most faithfully deliver'd. He perfectly acquitted himself with some important commissions I gave him and appears to me entitled to every reward his situation can admit of. Done under my hand, Richmond

November 21st 1784

Lafayette

The next time James petitioned the House of Delegates, he attached Lafayette's testimonial to his petition:

To the honorable the Speaker & gentlemen of the genl Assembly,

The petition of James (a slave belonging to Will: Armistead of New Kent county) humbly sheweth:

That your petitioner perswaded of the just right which all mankind have to Freedom, notwithstanding his own state of bondage, with an honest desire to serve this Country in its defence thereof, did, during the ravages of Lord Cornwallis thro' this state, . . . enter into the service of the Marquiss Lafayette. . . . For proof of the above your petitioner begs leave to refer to the certificate of the Marquiss Lafayette hereto annexed, & after taking his case as here stated into consideration he humbly intreats that he may be granted that Freedom, which he flatters himself he has in some degree contributed to establish. . . .

This time, the delegates acted in James's favor:

I. WHEREAS it is represented that James, a negro slave . . . did . . . enter into the service of the Marquis la Fayette, and at the peril of his life . . . faithfully executed important commissions entrusted to him by the marquis; and the said James hath made application to this assembly to set him free ... which it is judged reasonable and right to do.

II. *Be it therefore enacted,* That the said James shall, from and after the passing of this act, enjoy as full freedom as if he had been born free. . . .

And so, on January 9, 1787, James became a free man. He picked up the pen to sign his emancipation papers. He had always been known by one name, but when he wrote his name for the first time as a free man, he chose to honor the person who had played such an important role in obtaining his freedom. He signed his name *James Lafayette.*

14

New Life, New Name

James Lafayette was thirty-nine years old, and his new life was just beginning. He bought forty acres of land near the plantation on which he had grown up. He farmed the land with his wife and children. Along with other workers, they tilled and sowed the land.

The harder James worked, the freer he felt. He knew that the fruits of his labor belonged to himself and his family. It was a feeling like no other. James and his family spent many happy years farming.

By 1818, old age kept James from performing the hard labor required to maintain a farm. Once again, he petitioned the Virginia assembly. Four decades after he had asked lawmakers to grant him his freedom, the seventy-year-old former spy asked to receive a soldier's pension.

James's request was granted in recognition of the service he had provided for his country at its founding. James was given sixty dollars immediately, to be followed by a yearly sum of forty dollars (about a thousand dollars today).

James left his farm and traveled to Richmond twice a year to collect his pension, which was given to him in two twenty-dollar payments. James became a familiar figure in Richmond. A local newspaper referred to him as "a very <u>venerable</u> and respectable free black man."

James enjoyed his trips to the city. It was a time for him and the other "old timers" to share war stories and remembrances. James never tired of sharing his memories of the Marquis de Lafayette. Even though decades had passed, the memories had not faded.

On one of his trips to Richmond, James learned that Lafayette, the last living general of the Revolutionary War, had been invited to tour the United States for the upcoming fiftieth anniversary of American independence. What wonderful news! Could it be possible that after so many years, James would get to see his dear friend again?

venerable: deserving of respect

15

Reunion

From August 1824 to September 1825, James's hero, the Marquis de Lafayette, would tour all of the now twenty-four states. And in October 1824, the marquis would make stops in Yorktown and Richmond, Virginia.

Among those traveling with Lafayette was his son, Georges Washington Lafayette, who had been named after Lafayette's own hero.

Everywhere Lafayette appeared, he was greeted by huge, cheering crowds. When he returned to Yorktown, the location of the decisive battle of the revolution, the crowd was as massive and adoring as any he had encountered.

And in that crowd was James. He was determined to see his old commander, even if only from afar. After all, Lafayette was one of the most famous men in the world. He had come to meet with <u>dignitaries</u> and presidents. Who was James but an elderly man in the crowd?

James waited along with the hundreds of others who had come out to see the beloved Frenchman. Finally,

dignitaries: honored people

the <u>ornate</u> carriage in which the marquis rode came into view. As it rolled past him, James caught sight of the marquis! James was thrilled. He had accomplished his mission.

Then, all of a sudden, the carriage came to a halt. The marquis himself stepped out. Having recognized James, the marquis headed straight to him. Recovering from his surprise, James remembered his French from long ago and said, "Bonjour, mon ami."

The two men embraced. They were not then a former slave and a celebrated general. They had both lived extraordinary lives, and they were equals. In that moment, the seventy-six-year-old black man and the elderly white man felt the joy of seeing each other again, the bond that their experience of half a century before had created, and the sadness of a final farewell.

"Adieu, mon ami."

"Adieu."

Lafayette climbed back into his carriage. James returned to his farm. His brief reunion with Lafayette was written about in newspapers. This brought James a bit of <u>notoriety</u>. The artist John B. Martin, in a fitting tribute, painted a portrait of a gray-haired James. The former spy died at the age of eighty-two, a free citizen of the country he had helped create.

---

ornate: fancily decorated
notoriety: fame

When Americans celebrate Independence Day, they should recall the spy who risked everything to see the nation come into being. When they acknowledge the freedom they cherish, they should not overlook the enslaved man who fought for that freedom. And every time they honor the heroes of the American Revolution, they should remember his name—James Lafayette.

Discussion Questions

1. Give two examples of how James's life was different from the lives of other enslaved children on the plantation.

2. Why was tobacco an important crop in colonial Virginia? Give two reasons.

3. Why did James not want to work in the tobacco fields?

4. What do you think might have been the hardest part about being an enslaved child?

5. How was James' life similar to that of the plantation owner's son? How was James's life different?

6. James longed to be free. What did he think would be the best thing about being free?

7. Why did the Americans want to break away from Great Britain and become an independent country?

8. What are two events that happened that made King George III send Redcoats to the American colonies?

9. When did the American Revolution begin? When did the United States become an independent country?

10. Who were the Loyalists? Who were the Patriots?

11. What was the main reason that black people fought in the Revolutionary War?

12. Why did some African Americans fight for the British?

13. Why did James choose to serve on the American side?

14. Who was the Marquis de Lafayette? Why did James admire him?

15. What was the job of a spy? Why was it such a dangerous job?

16. What do you think would be important personality traits for a spy?

17. What reward did James believe he would receive for being a spy for the Americans?

18. What are two pieces of useful information that James found out through spying that he was able to give to Lafayette?

19. Soon after becoming a spy, James became a double agent. What is a double agent?

20. Thanks to James, the traitor Benedict Arnold was almost captured. Why did the attempt to capture

Benedict Arnold fail?

21. The Battle of Yorktown decided the final outcome of the Revolutionary War. What part did James play in this battle?

22. Why was James still enslaved even after the Americans won the war?

23. Do you think a spy should have received the same reward as a soldier? Why or why not?

24. James did not give up. What did he do after the war to continue his fight for freedom?

25. How did the Marquis de Lafayette help James in this new effort to gain his freedom?

26. At what age did James finally gain his freedom? What did James do when he became free?

27. Why did James add "Lafayette" to his name?

28. Is there someone in your life who has helped you achieve a goal? How can you honor that person?

29. The French have two words for goodbye. What does *au revoir* mean? What does *adieu* mean?

Meet the Author

Glenda Armand has had a long career as a teacher, school librarian, and author. Her work has allowed her to fulfill her love of learning, reading, writing, and teaching children. She enjoys writing picture book biographies that inspire children to dream big.

She is the author of the award-winning *Love Twelve Miles Long*, a book about the young Frederick Douglass, who was born a slave and grew up to become a renowned abolitionist and friend to Abraham Lincoln. Ms. Armand has also written two books on gifted Shakespearean actor Ira Aldridge, *Ira's Shakespeare Dream* and *The Story of Trailblazing Actor Ira Aldridge*.

Her most recent books are *Song in a Rainstorm: The Story of Musical Prodigy Thomas "Blind Tom" Wiggins* and *Black Leaders in the Civil Rights Movement.*

She has books coming soon on African American foodways, the Great Migration, and Augustus Jackson, the "Father of Ice Cream."

Ms. Armand has a son who is a musician and athlete and a daughter who is a nurse. When not writing or practicing the piano, Ms. Armand tends a garden full of roses and succulents.

Drop by her website at *glenda-armand.com.*

Meet the Illustrator

Kailien Singson. A born artist, Kailien hails from the northeastern region of India known for its rich natural beauty that serves as a constant inspiration in his work. His passion for art began at a young age with artistic scribbles in notebooks at school, and gradually developed into a serious career that led him to pursue a degree in Arts. Having explored several techniques in art through his education and professional years in publishing, Kailien specializes in using striking colors, and depicting realistic forms in his work. He is equally adept at digital and traditional art styles, taking inspiration from everyday life.

Credits

Cover Illustration by
Kailien Singson & Ivan Pesic

Title Page Illustration by
Kailien Singson

Text Illustrations by
In Courtesy of Glenda Armand / 58
In Courtesy of Kailien Singson / 60
Kailien Singson / 10, 20, 25, 26, 28, 30, 32, 38, 40, 41